Are There Contradictions In the Bible?

Ralph O. Muncaster

HARVEST HOUSE PUBLISHERS
Eugene, Oregon 97402

Cover by Terry Dugan Design, Minneapolis, Minnesota

By Ralph O. Muncaster

Can Archaeology Prove the New Testament?
Can Archaeology Prove the Old Testament?
Can We Know for Certain We Are Going to Heaven?
Can You Trust the Bible?
Creation vs. Evolution
Creation vs. Evolution Video
Does Prayer Really Work?
Does the Bible Predict the Future?
How to Talk About Jesus with the Skeptics in Your Life
How Do We Know Jesus Is God?
Is the Bible Really a Message from God?
Science—Was the Bible Ahead of Its Time?
What Is the Proof for the Resurrection?
How Is Jesus Different from Other Religious Leaders?
What Is the Trinity?
What Really Happened Christmas Morning?
What Really Happens When You Die?
Why Does God Allow Suffering?
Why Are Scientists Turning to God?

ARE THERE CONTRADICTIONS IN THE BIBLE?
Examine the Evidence Series

Copyright © 2002 by Ralph O. Muncaster
Published by Harvest House Publishers
Eugene, Oregon 97402

Library of Congress Cataloging-in-Publication Data

Muncaster, Ralph O.
    Are there contradictions in the Bible? / Ralph O. Muncaster.
        p. cm. — (Examine the evidence)
    Includes bibliographical references.
    ISBN 0-7369-0774-2
        1. Bible—Evidences, authority, etc. I. Title

BS480 .M743 2002
220.1—dc21   2001051573

Printed in the United States of America.

02 03 04 05 06 07 / BP–GB / 10 9 8 7 6 5 4 3 2 1

Contents

Countering Biblical Contradiction Claims 4

The Key Issues 5

Defining Contradictions 6

The Importance of Similarities and Differences 8

Genesis 1 vs. Genesis 2 10

The Importance of Biblical Names 12

The Names of God 14

Inconsistency of Names 16

Is the Old Testament God Different
   Than the New Testament God? 18

How to Analyze Contradictions 22

Contradiction in Jesus' Ancestry? 24

Sequencing Problems? 26

Contradictory Dates and Times for the Crucifixion? 28

Contradictions About the Resurrection? 32

Other Suspected Contradictions 36

Common Questions 45

Notes 48

Bibliography 48

Countering Biblical Contradiction Claims

Some people claim that the Bible has a lot of contradictions within. Yet it continues to be a source of inspiration and the foundation of the Christian faith after more than 2000 years. Are there really contradictions?

If God truly inspired all the books of the Bible, He would certainly not contradict Himself. Yet we also know that people actually wrote the Bible. Did the human authors make mistakes? Did they misunderstand God's inspiration in some cases? Or did mistakes creep in later during copying and translating? In the case of apparent contradictions, is it possible we aren't digging deep enough to really understand the message?

Since Christians claim the Bible is inspired by God, it is important to establish that it doesn't contain contradictions. Why?

1. Otherwise, how can the Bible be trusted?
2. How do people know which parts of the Bible to believe or not to believe?
3. A contradictory Bible allows "picking and choosing" what to follow regarding its messages and truths.

When people research supposed contradictions in the Bible, they find that the God of the Bible is *still perfect* on all issues despite thousands of years of copying and translating. Does that mean today's Bibles are word-for-word perfect if they could be placed against the originals? No, because the originals were written in different languages. For instance, the original Hebrew Bible contains no vowels. Is the Bible inerrant? Absolutely. Except for very few variants in punctuation and letter choice, today's Bible accurately reflects God's inspiration.

This book will deal with the most commonly cited and important "contradictions."

The Key Issues

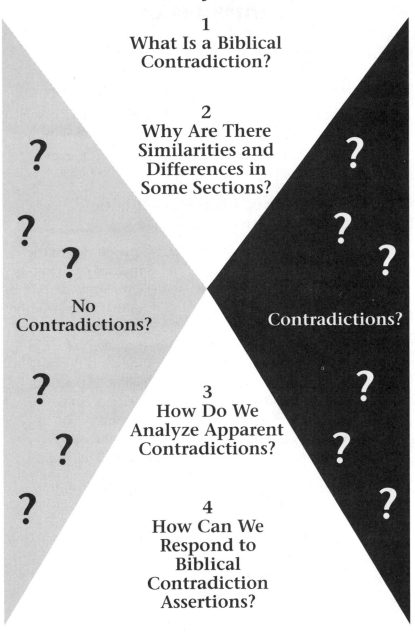

1
What Is a Biblical
Contradiction?

2
Why Are There
Similarities and
Differences in
Some Sections?

No
Contradictions?

Contradictions?

3
How Do We
Analyze Apparent
Contradictions?

4
How Can We
Respond to
Biblical
Contradiction
Assertions?

Defining Contradictions

What constitutes a biblical "contradiction"?
Webster defines "contradiction" as:

Contradiction: *Something containing contradictory elements.*

Contradictory: *Either of two propositions related in such a way that it is impossible for both to be true or both to be false.*[1]

So when dealing with the Bible, the "something" that must contain "contradictory elements" is the Bible itself.

Why Not Consider Outside Contradictions?

Other books in the Examine the Evidence series deal with the Bible and the issues of proof, claims, and supposed contradictions. (See copyright page for a list of titles.) For instance, *Can Archaeology Prove the Old Testament?* indicates that all previously held beliefs by "higher critics" of the Bible (a movement started in the late 1800s) have been proven false by modern archaeology. This includes previously held beliefs such as: 1) the early Hittites couldn't have existed in Abraham's time, 2) the "supposed" nondomestication of camels, 3) the strength of Lot's doors. The list goes on and on. All were later proven false by modern archaeology to such an extent that the Bible is used as an important history book for archaeologists of all religions.[2]

Science—Was the Bible Ahead of Its Time? points out the many references to scientific issues in the Bible that are 100 percent correct, even though they were written 2000 years before we "officially" discovered them! Among the Bible's foresights are principles of quarantine, proper sanitation, currents in the sea, the hydrologic cycle, and physics.[3]

Internal Biblical Consistency

Notice that by the Webster definition, within a source there needs to be at least *two* propositions where it would be *impossible* for both to be true or both to be false. In dealing with our analysis of what is and isn't consistent, we will review several of the most troubling "inconsistencies" that have been pointed out by biblical critics for centuries. The test will be clear impossibility—or at least the extreme unlikelihood—of alternate explanations. We will ask the following essential questions:

1. Is it impossible for the propositions in question to both be true?

2. Is it impossible for the propositions in question to both be false?

3. Is the original language misunderstood? Does it allow latitude?

4. Are there other possible explanations for the alleged inconsistency?

The Importance of Similarities and Differences

Some sections of the Bible, most notably the gospel accounts of Jesus, contain similarities and differences of the same event. Do these constitute contradictions? Not necessarily. In fact, there is a benefit to having both similarities and differences in eyewitness accounts:

Eyewitness Group 1 Accounts

Witness 1: "A lady was hit by a truck. Two men watched on the sidewalk. One was about 5'10" and wore a black shirt; the other was tall and wore a red shirt."

Witness 2: "A lady was hit by a truck. Two men watched on the sidewalk. One was about 5'10" and wore a black shirt; the other was tall and wore a red shirt."

Witness 3: "A lady was hit by a truck. Two men watched on the sidewalk. One was about 5'10" and wore a black shirt; the other was tall and wore a red shirt."

Eyewitness Group 2 Accounts:

Witness 1: "A lady was hit by a truck. A man rushed out to see if she was okay. He was about 5'10" and wore black. It occurred at 12:00."

Witness 2: "A lady was hit by a truck. Two men watched on the sidewalk. One was about 5'10" and wore a black shirt; the other was tall and wore a red shirt. It occurred about noon."

Witness 3: "A lady was hit by a truck. Several witnessed it. The paramedics were the first to arrive. I looked at my watch; it was 12:02."

Which group more fully describes the events? The first "cookie cutter" group provides less credible information because the information is identical. Perhaps there was collusion for some purpose. Although different, the second group is not inconsistent. The similarities indicate corroboration (support) for the fundamentals of the event. The differences add depth, meaning, and insight.

The real story: Slightly before 12:00 a lady was hit by a truck. There were several witnesses, including two men. One was about 5'10" and wore a black shirt. The other was a tall man wearing a red shirt. The one wearing black rushed out to see if the lady was okay. The paramedics were the first officials to arrive at 12:02.

Notice the importance of both similarities and differences for a trustworthy and complete account!

Genesis 1 vs. Genesis 2

Some critics claim that Genesis 1 is inconsistent with Genesis 2 regarding the order of creation.

Basis for Claimed Contradiction

1. Genesis 2:5-7 seems to indicate that man was created before vegetation.

2. Genesis 1:12 indicates vegetation was created on day 3; Genesis 1:27 indicates man and woman were created on day 6.

1. Genesis 2:7,19 seem to indicate that animals were created after mankind.

2. Genesis 1:20-25 indicates animals were created on days 5 and 6 and in Genesis 1:26,27, the Bible indicates man and woman were created later on day 6.

Response to Contradiction Claim

Genesis 1 is clearly a methodical account of Creation. We know this from the opening words "In the beginning" and by the methodical system of steps or "days" each highlighted with "bookends" that mark the beginning and ending (evening and morning). It describes exactly what happened on each day.

Genesis 2 has an entirely different purpose. It discusses what happened to heaven and earth *once they were created*, with particular emphasis on the creation of mankind, which is the focal point of God's Word.

Many scholars approach Genesis 1 and 2 as a single unit, with Genesis 1 providing chronological details and Genesis 2 adding complementary information. Genesis 2 focuses on the details that relate to humanity's relationship with God and His creation. For instance, "God planted a garden" doesn't rule out the possibility that other vegetation had already been formed. The phrase could be referring to a special place God created for the man and woman to live.

Where Did Cain Get His Wife?

Some ask where Cain, the first son of Adam, got his wife. Genesis 4:17 states that "Cain lay with his wife, and she became pregnant and gave birth to Enoch." Yet up to this point, no potential females have been mentioned.

The Bible states that Adam had other sons and daughters beyond Cain, Abel, and Seth (who was born when Adam was 130 years old) (Genesis 5:4). Seth, in turn, also had sons and daughters (Genesis 5:7). Considering the long life spans, Cain had plenty of time to take a wife from either Adam or Seth's daughters.

Conclusion

There is no contradiction between Genesis 1 and 2. Genesis 1 is chronological; Genesis 2 complements Genesis 1 by adding more details and focusing on how man and woman relate to God and creation.

The Importance of Biblical Names

Today, names are given for a number of reasons: 1) to honor ancestors, 2) to honor relatives, 3) because of an attraction to a celebrity, 4) because it "sounds nice," and many other reasons. Seldom in the western world is a name given to someone with the importance given in biblical times. Back then, names were given for a purpose. They were considered equivalent to the person with the name and often represented a person's reputation. In fact, even the word "name" is often translated to mean "reputation" (Mark 6:14; Revelation 3:1). Another example is in 1 Samuel 25:25: ". . . Nabal. He is just like his name—his name is Fool, and folly goes with him."

So important are names of individuals, that the word "name" appears more than 1000 times in the Bible.

Name Changes

Name changes were often made, noted usually to provide a "promotion." For example, when Jacob was wrestling with God (manifest in the form of a person) and requested a blessing, he was rewarded with a name change to Israel (Genesis 32:28).

Even today, orthodox Jews (those who strictly adhere to the literal words of the Torah) will often change someone's name when he approaches death in hopes of healing or a new life.[4]

Prayer in Jesus' Name

Believing in Jesus' name is tantamount to believing in Jesus Himself. John 3:18 states clearly that those not believing in Jesus' name are condemned because they don't believe in Him.

Therefore, prayer in Jesus' name is not a ritualistic or mystical formula. It is a statement of belief in Jesus as the Savior. When said at the end of a prayer, it presumes that all preceding it is based on the desire to serve and please God.

God Gives Names

Several times in the Bible, *God* changed the names of people.[5] In some cases (such as Jacob), God is represented by a theophany (a manifestation of God through a being):

- Abram became "exalted father"
- Sarai became "princess"
- Jacob became "may God protect"
- Isaac means "he laughs" (Genesis 17:19)
- John, prescribed for John the Baptist, "God shows favor" (Luke 1:13)
- Simeon (Simon) to "hearing"
- Jesus, prescribed for Jesus the Christ, "Savior" (Luke 1:31)

- Abraham (Genesis 17:5) "father of multitudes"
- Sarah (Genesis 17:15) "princess"
- Israel means "he strives with God" (Genesis 32:28)
- Peter means "the rock" (John 1:42)

The Names of God

Basis for Claimed Inconsistency

Some have claimed that the change in the identifying names of God in Genesis 1 (*Elohym*), Genesis 2 (*Yahweh*), and elsewhere in the Bible (*Jehovah*, etc.) indicate an inconsistent God.

Response to Contradiction Claim

The first key to understanding the names of God is understanding the importance placed on names. God's name was (and is) more than a label. It reflects God Himself. Exodus 6:3 indicates this: *"I appeared to Abraham, to Isaac and to Jacob as God Almighty, but by my name the LORD I did not make myself known to them."*

In essence what this means is that God appeared to the patriarchs as God Almighty *(El Shaddai)*, not the miraculous, covenant-keeping God who was about to deliver His people from bondage (Exodus 5:2).

So important was the name of God at the time the Bible was originally written, that it is referred to in the third commandment: "You shall not misuse the name of the LORD your God" (Exodus 20:7). When copies of the Old Testament were made, scribes omitted specific letters to avoid using the LORD's name in vain. They also said a sanctification prayer before writing it down.

The vastness of God requires a large set of names with various meanings to provide the respect and reputation He is due.[6,7]

Names of God

- *Elohim* (Elohym)—"God of Majesty"—emphasizing Him as Creator of all things

- *El*—the root of the word for God

- *El* Elyon—"God most high" (over all things)

- *El* Shaddai—"God Almighty" (all powerful)

- *El-Eloe-Yisrael*—"God of Jacob" (or "God of Israel")

- *Yaweh* (spelled YHWH in early Hebrew)—"LORD" (represents God's personal character)

- *I AM, LORD*—defines the "personal" Yaweh as the same God as that of the patriarchs (Exodus 3:13-16). Jesus later referred to Himself as such (John 8:58)

- *Jehovah*—derivations of Yaweh

    Jehovah-jiru—"The LORD Will Provide"

    Jehovah-nissi—"The LORD Is Peace"

    Jehovah-shammah—"The LORD Is There"

    Jehovah-tsebaoth—"The LORD of Hosts"

    Jehovah Elohe Yisrael—"The LORD God of Israel"

- *Abba*—"Daddy" or "Dear Father"

- *Adonai*—"LORD and Father" or, more generally, "LORD" in the Old Testament

Inconsistency of Names

There are several supposed discrepancies in referring to some people. As reviewed earlier, many of these are easily traceable to name changes that were used to "promote" (and occasionally "demote") people. Listed below are commonly cited examples and their explanations.

1. *The correct father of Jotham?* Matthew 1:9, in the genealogy of Jesus, states, "Uzziah the father of Jotham" (Uzziah is Greek). However, in the Old Testament Azariah is referred to as Jotham's father (2 Kings 15:1-7, 1 Chronicles 3:12). Later in 2 Kings, he is referred to as Uzziah (15:32,34). Likewise he was referred to elsewhere as Uzziah (2 Chronicles 26; 27:2; Isaiah 1:1; 6:1; 7:1). This is a classic case of an individual bearing two names that are similar in meaning. Azariah means "God has helped." Uzziah means "God is my strength."

2. *Zechariah, son of Berekiah, the last martyr?* Jesus said Zechariah son of Berekiah was the last martyr of the Old Testament (Matthew 23:34,35). Most people assume that the last martyr was Zechariah, son of Jehoiada, who was stoned in the Temple court as ordered by King Joash (2 Chronicles 24:20-22). However, there were many martyrs since Zechariah ben Jehoiada, who died circa 800 B.C. In fact, the last martyr mentioned in Scripture is Zechariah, son of Berekiah, just as Jesus indicated (Zechariah 1:1).

3. *Who came to Jesus, a centurion or Jewish elders?* According to Matthew 8:5-13, a centurion approached Jesus directly to request the healing of his sick servant. Luke 7:2 says that some elders of the Jews were sent. It would not be uncommon for a Roman centurion to send Jews, familiar with the culture of Jesus, to request the healing first, then make a direct personal request.

4. *Who approached Jesus about James and John?* Matthew 20:20,21 indicates that the mother of James and John came to Jesus to request preferential treatment after He comes into His kingdom. Mark 10:35 states that it was James and John themselves. Similar to question 3, it would not be unusual during those days for a mother and her children to agree on such a request and then have the mother present it first, followed by the sons.

5. *What did the centurion and soldiers say at Jesus' death?* Both Matthew 27:54 and Mark 15:39 indicate that the soldiers exclaimed the same thing: "Surely He was the son of God." The only difference between the two is that Mark identified a particular centurion (at the foot of the cross) and said "this man" in place of "He." Luke 23:47, on the other hand, indicated a single centurion saying, "Surely this was a righteous man."

   This is certainly easy to reconcile considering the events going on around Jesus—utter darkness, an earthquake, tombs opening with many holy people raised to life. There were several soldiers and one could easily imagine them all being impressed enough to exclaim various remarks that each of the gospel writers might have heard.

Is the Old Testament God Different Than . . .

Many people think the God of the Old Testament is significantly different than the God of the New Testament. To some, this is so troubling that they refuse to trust the Bible at all. To others, it provides an excuse to not consider the importance of the teachings in the Old Testament. Are there two different Gods? Did God's nature change?

Basis for Contradiction Claim

The Old Testament is filled with examples of God's wrath and judgment, which directly contrasts with the loving, forgiving God of the New Testament.

Examples of Old Testament Wrath

- Expelling Adam and Eve out of Eden and causing great hardship and death simply for eating an apple (Genesis 3:16-19,22,23)
- Killing all inhabitants of the earth (including children) with a great flood for evil that generally existed (Genesis 6–8)
- Destroying Sodom and Gomorrah (including children) for evil of adults (Genesis 19)
- Killing the first-born children of the Egyptians because of an unyielding Pharaoh (Exodus 11:5)
- Killing Aaron's sons Nadab and Abihu because they offered "unauthorized fire" before the Lord (Leviticus10:1,2)
- Striking the Israelites with a plague because of their grumbling for quail to eat (Numbers 11:4,20,33)
- Destroying Korah, Dathan, and Abiram, along with 250 men, for rebelling against Moses and Aaron (Numbers 16)
- Ordering the Israelites to "take vengeance" on the

. . . the New Testament God?

Midianites for worship of Baal, including killing all boys and every woman "who has slept with a man" (Numbers 31:1,11-18)

- Destroying every living thing—men, women, children, and animals in the city of Jericho—except Rahab, who helped the spies (Joshua 6:21)

These are but a few examples of God's wrath poured out as the Israelites took over the land promised to them by God.

Examples of New Testament Forgiveness

The God of the New Testament, in the person of Jesus Christ, preached love and forgiveness.

- "Do not resist an evil person" (Matthew 5:39)
- "Love one another. As I have loved you, so you must love one another" (John 13:34)
- ". . . If you hold anything against anyone, forgive him" (Mark 11:25)

How Can These Differences Be Reconciled?

It is important to understand the status and objectives for spiritual development of the Israelites/Jews in each setting. In the Old Testament, God is *revealing His nature* to the Israelites and *preparing them for a Savior* to come (who will eventually lead them to eternal life). In the New Testament, God *has revealed the Savior* and *is offering eternal life*. God hasn't changed, but the environment has. The teaching emphasis moved from the temporal to the eternal.

God's Nature

God's nature is comprised of three basic parts: 1) He is perfectly holy (Leviticus 11:45; Revelation 4:8), 2) He is perfectly just (Deuteronomy 32:4; 2 Thessalonians 1:6), and He is perfectly loving (Deuteronomy 7:9; 1 John 4:16). Notice that this fundamental nature of God is included in *both* the New and Old Testaments. Further inspection will reveal hundreds of such examples.

These parts of God's nature cannot always be fulfilled concurrently on earth in a way humankind understands. For example, a perfectly holy God might need a pagan land purged of sin, even if it means innocent children might suffer. (This seems to contradict love from a human standpoint.) Yet God is also perfectly just and can deal with such human-perspective injustices in an eternal stage (after death).

Response to Contradiction Claim

Apart from the equal nature of God just noted, we find that, proportionally, there seems to be an equal number of examples of the wrath of God and love of God in both Testaments. (Since the Old Testament is longer, it contains more of each.)

Examples of New Testament Wrath

- "Whoever believes in the Son has eternal life, but whoever rejects the Son will not see life, for God's wrath remains on him" (John 3:36)
- "The wrath of God is being revealed from heaven against all the godlessness and wickedness of men who suppress the truth by their wickedness" (Romans 1:18)
- "Put to death, therefore, whatever belongs to your earthly nature: sexual immorality, impurity, lust, evil desires, and greed, which is idolatry. Because of these, the wrath of God is coming" (Colossians 3:5,6)
- "God remembered Babylon the Great and gave her the cup filled with the wine of the fury of his wrath" (Revelation 16:19)
- "They will weed out of his kingdom everything that causes sin and all who do evil. They will throw them into the fiery furnace, where there will be weeping and gnashing of teeth" (Matthew 13:41,42)
- "The angels will come and separate the wicked from the righteous and throw them into the fiery furnace, where there will be weeping and gnashing of teeth" (Matthew 13:49,50)

Examples of God's Love in the Old Testament

- ". . . The compassionate and gracious God, slow to anger, abounding in love" (Exodus 34:6)
- ". . . He is the faithful God, keeping his covenant of love" (Deuteronomy 7:9)
- "But you, O Lord, are a compassionate and gracious God . . . abounding in love and faithfulness" (Psalm 86:15)

The Old and New Testaments are based on the same God.

How to Analyze Contradictions

Issue

Step 1—Overview State in simple terms the alleged contradiction.	Gen. 1 appears to contradict Gen. 2 in the sequence of creation events
Step 2—Definition List all key elements that indicate a conflict.	Summarize the verses and claims of each issue
Step 3—Hypothesis State all potential means of resolving the conflict.	1. Address intent of each 2. Address language of each
Step 4—Research Research necessary areas. This may include original languages, culture, and sentence structure.	1. Review each side carefully for context and content 2. Research words and tense of words in each proposition
Step 5—Judge Decide if any alternative explanation is plausible. Remember, the test is for *impossibility* of resolution.	There were two separate purposes for Gen. 1 and 2
Step 6—Conclude Reach a conclusion according to the definition of contradiction.	There is *no contradiction* in the order of creation between Gen. 1 and 2

Genesis 1	Genesis 2
Gen. 1 says both vegetation and animals were created before mankind	Gen. 2 seems to indicate creation of mankind prior to discussion of vegetation and livestock

Specifics	Specifics
—V. 12 indicates vegetation was created on day 3	—Vv. 7, 8 indicate the creation of man and woman
—Vv. 20-25 indicate animals were created on day 5 and 6 (early)	—Vv. 9, 10 indicate trees and a garden planted
—V. 27 indicates man and woman were created on day 6	—V. 19 indicates animals and birds created

Proposition A	Proposition B
Because Gen. 2 reveals creation of vegetation, beasts, and birds *after* man and Gen. 1 clearly states their creation *before* man, they are in conflict	1. Perhaps Gen. 2 complements Gen. 1 instead of presenting Creation again
	2. Perhaps the language provides latitude for the difference. Perhaps perspective can harmonize both accounts

Purpose	Purpose
Gen. 1 provides the basic structure of the creation of the universe	Gen. 2 complements Gen. 1 by providing details of God's creation of mankind and how He prepared the earth for the first humans

Context	Context
Gen. 1 is clearly a chronological overview of creation itself	The context of Gen. 2 is clearly focused on mankind's creation and place in relation to God and His creation

Contradiction in Jesus' Ancestry?

Why is the ancestry of Jesus, from David on, reported differently in Matthew and Luke? Genealogies were important to the Jews for many reasons, not the least of which included property rights. So how could two biblical authors be at such odds?

LUKE 3,		MATTHEW 1,
David		David
Nathan	2 Sam. 12:24-25;	Solomon
Mattatha	1 Ch. 3:5; 14:4; 23:1;	
Menan	2 Ch. 1:12; 1 Ki. 11:1	
Melea	1 Ki. 11:43; 14:21;	Rehoboam
Eliakim	2 Ch. 12:13	
Jon	1 Ki. 14:31;	Abijah
Joseph	2 Ch. 11:20; 13:21	
Juda	1 Ki. 15:8-24	Asa
Simeon	2 Ch. 15:17; 16:12	
Levi	1 Ki. 15:24; 22:41-50	Jehoshaphat
Matthat	2 Ch. 20:35-37	
Jorim	1 Ki. 22:50; 2 Ki. 8:16	Jehoram
Eliezer	2 Ch. 21:14-20	
Jose	2 Ki. 8:24-29; 9:16;	Ahaziah
Er	10:13; 2 Ch. 22:9	
Elmodam	2 Ki. 11:21; 12:1; 13:1	Joash
Cosam	2 Ki. 12:21; 14:13	Amaziah
Addi	2 Ki. 14:21; 15:1-27	Uzziah
Melchi	2 Ki. 15:5,30	Jotham
Neri	2 Ch. 3:12; Is. 7:1	
Salathiel	2 Ki. 15:38; Is. 7:1	Ahaz
Zerubbabel	2 Ki. 18:1; 5:7	Hezekiah
Rhesa	1 Ch. 3:13; Is. 37:1	
Joanna	2 Ki. 21:1; 1 Ch. 3:132	Manasseh
Juda	2 Ki. 21:19; 1 Ch. 3:13	Amon
Joseph	1 Ki. 13:2; 2 Ki. 21:24	Josiah
Semei	2 Ki. 23:34; 24:1-7	Jehoiakim
Mattathias	Jer. 1:3,25; 2 Ch. 36:4	
Maath	2 Ki. 24:6; 25:27	Jehoiachin
Nagge	2 Ch. 36:4; Jer. 22:24	
Esli	1 Ch. 3:17,19	Salathiel
Naum	Ez. 3:2,8; Ne. 12:1	Zerubbabel
Amos	Ha. 1:1,12,14; 2:2	
Mattathias	Mt. 1:13	Abiud
Joseph	Mt. 1:13	Eliakim
Janna	Mt. 1:13	Azor
Melchi	Mt. 1:14	Sadoc
Levi	Mt. 1:14	Achim
Matthat	Mt. 1:14	Eliud
Heli	Mt. 1:15	Eleazar
	Mt. 1:15	Matthan
	Mt. 1:16	Jacob
Joseph	Mt. 1:16	Joseph (husband of Mary)
(Son-in-Law)		

Response to Contradiction

Luke

The genealogy cited in Luke was based on Mary, the human side of Jesus. Matthew was the more common genealogy given through the line of the males to Joseph, husband of Mary. This is not surprising since Luke was a physician who dealt with human problems and Matthew was a tax collector who dealt with legal issues (transferred through males). Jesus was the legal heir.

There is evidence of this in the Greek. In the case of Luke, verse 3:23 provides a clue when it includes the words: "He was the son, *so it was thought*, of Joseph." This calls attention to the only human parent—Mary.

Matthew

This genealogy deals strictly with the *legal* line down through Joseph. The Greek word for begot, "egnnesen," is used in the entire genealogy from Abraham to Joseph. However Joseph is not said to have begotten Jesus. Instead the Greek calls Joseph the "husband of Mary."[8]

This genealogy ends with Heli as the father-in-law of Joseph, the legal heir.

There is no contradiction. Both Jesus' human and legal lines are provided.

Sequencing Problems?

Some people are troubled by the different sequencing of various events, such as the temptations of Jesus, the fig tree incident, and the issue of the entry and exit into Jericho.

Temptations of Jesus

Matthew 4:5-7 indicates that the second temptation of Jesus is Satan's enticement to jump from the pinnacle of the Temple—relying on God's angels to save Him. Luke 4:5-12 makes the temptation of "world empire" number two and the pinnacle temptation number three. How can this be reconciled?

Recognizing that we have different authors, each with a different degree of interest in various temptations and their importance, it would be natural for each author to represent them in a different order. Chronology is not important. Just like a court of law today, witnesses often relate different events in different time frames—unless chronology becomes an issue. As indicated on pp. 8–9, the fact that there are similarities and differences adds strength to the testimony, not weakness.

Fig Tree

Following Palm Sunday, Matthew makes it clear that Jesus went straight to the Temple to expel the "money changers" (Matthew 21:10-12). He does not speak of "cursing the fig tree" until verse 18. Mark, on the other hand, seems to indicate that the "Temple incident" occurred after the cursing of the fig tree (Mark 11:12-16). This appears to be a direct contradiction.

Resolving this apparent problem requires understanding the typical writing style of the authors. *Matthew* tended to write in a topical sense, placing importance on topics at the expense of strict chronology. This is evident in his writing about the Sermon on the Mount, which was undoubtedly given over a period of time in many settings. *Mark*, on the other hand, tended to write a strict chronology of events. Both Matthew and Mark do agree that Jesus went immediately to the Temple upon his arrival on Palm Sunday (Matthew 21:12; Mark 11:11). (Mark says that Jesus "looked around in indignation," and then returned to Bethany.) They also agree that the cursing of the fig tree occurred the day after Jesus' entry into Jerusalem, when He was on His way back to the Temple.

Entering or Leaving Jericho?

Matthew 20:29 indicates that Jesus and His disciples were leaving Jericho when He healed two blind men. Mark 10:46,47 agrees with the leaving of Jericho but mentions only one blind man. Luke mentions one blind man but indicates Jesus was entering Jericho.

The issue of whether it was one or two blind men can be easily dealt with in respect to the importance of similarities and differences in the Bible, with different authors emphasizing different things. Mark names the blind man (Bartimaeus), and Luke indicates a "certain blind man," indicating that one had some distinction.

Archaeology[9] has answered the entering–leaving issue. During the time of Jesus there was an "old Jericho" and a "new Jericho." Jesus was simply going from one to the other.[7]

Contradictory Dates and Times . . .

In several cases critics have claimed there are contradictory dates and times in reference to the final week of Jesus' life on earth.

Alleged Contradictions

1. *How long was Jesus in the tomb?* Matthew states that Jesus would be dead and buried (metaphorically like Jonah in the whale) for 3 days and 3 nights (Matthew 12:40). Generally, people acknowledge Jesus was crucified on Friday before the Sabbath, which started at sunset on Friday. How can we arrive at three full days—let alone three full nights?

2. *Was the crucifixion on a Thursday or a Friday?* The synoptic gospels (Matthew, Mark, and Luke) seem to indicate a crucifixion the day before a Sabbath (generally starting at sunset on Friday).

3. *The hour in which Jesus was crucified.* Mark states Jesus was crucified at the "third hour" (Mark 15:25), while John indicates that the trial was still going on at the sixth hour (John 19:14).

In analyzing this entire scenario, it is valuable to research the role Jesus played.

Jesus as the Passover Lamb

Clearly, Jesus was identified as the passover lamb—from the beginning of His ministry until Revelation (the end of time). John 1:29 says,

> The next day John saw Jesus coming toward him and said, "Look, the Lamb of God, who takes away the sin of the world!"

. . . for the Crucifixion?

At the end of time, Revelation 21:22 states,

> I did not see a temple in the city, because the Lord God Almighty and the Lamb are its temple.

The parallel of Jesus as the perfect passover lamb is so strong that it is worth considering Old Testament law concerning Passover:

1. On the tenth of Nisan a perfect lamb is to be selected for slaughter (Exodus 12:3).

2. On the fourteenth of Nisan, Passover, the lamb is to be slaughtered (2 Chronicles 30:15).

3. The day after Passover was a "holy convocation day" or "special Sabbath" since it was the first day of the feast of unleavened bread (Leviticus 23:7-8). Hence, any day after the Passover would be a "special Sabbath"—it didn't need to be Saturday. John identifies it as such (John 19:31).

4. No bones would be broken in the Passover lamb (Numbers 9:12).

For Jesus to precisely meet this parallel as the "perfect passover lamb" several things had to happen:

1. He had to be "selected" on the tenth of Nisan (Palm Sunday).

2. He had to be crucified on the fourteenth of Nisan (Passover). This would be after sundown on Wednesday, which could be Thursday morning.

3. Because there was always a "holy convocation" day or "special Sabbath" after the Passover, the next day would always be a Sabbath. In Matthew 28:1, the word "Sabbath" in the Greek is plural.

4. No bones would be broken during Jesus' crucifixion as indicated (John 19:33).

Answers to "Day Contradictions"

- While the specific day is somewhat unknown, the result doesn't change. Most scholars hold to the traditional Friday crucifixion day on the basis of several things: First, they claim that "palm Sunday" was really "palm Monday." Second, they consider what John refers to as the "day of preparation" (for Passover [Greek "paraskeue"]) as coming into common parlance as Friday at the time.[10] This is important because, in some Bibles, the Gospel of John (19:14) indicates the trial of Jesus was on the day of preparation, not on Passover itself. It represents a translational difficulty. Was it Friday? Or was it the day of preparation? Finally, regarding the view on Matthew 12:40 ("as Jonah was three days and three nights in the belly of a huge fish"), scholars point out that Jewish use of idioms include part days as full days. Therefore, Friday, Saturday (Sabbath), and Sunday would constitute three days and three nights idiomatically.[11]

- Other scholars have a strong opinion for a Thursday crucifixion with an entry into Jerusalem on a Sunday (Palm Sunday). This would meet John's claim that the Last Supper was on a "day of preparation" (John 19:14). Assuming the tenth of Nisan fell on that Sunday, it would fit all criteria, including three days and three nights (Matthew 12:40).

"Hour Contradiction" Response

- Again, John's statement that it was the "Day of Preparation" at "about the sixth hour" when Jesus was still standing "trial" presents a possible contradiction (John 19:14), since the other gospels have Jesus being crucified at the third hour on Passover. This "Day of Preparation" can be reconciled in the original Greek in the context of the day. As previously mentioned, this phrase had come into common parlance to mean Friday. More importantly, since the Feast of Unleavened Bread was immediately on the heels of Passover, the day of Passover was essentially a day of preparation for the seven-day feast to follow.

- Then, as now, this period is commonly referred to as "Passover week." It was understood as such, so there was no need to insert "week" (sa-bua). The "preparation of Passover" could be understood as the Friday (or day before) Passover week.[11]

Conclusion

Though there remain some disputes about the precise timing of the crucifixion of Jesus, the possibility of reconciling those is within the realm of good scholarly evidence.

Contradictions About the Resurrection?

There are several supposed contradictions in the all-important account of the resurrection of Jesus.

Basis for Contradictions

1. How many women went to the tomb?
   a) Matthew says Mary Magdalene and the other Mary (Matthew 28:1)
   b) Mark says Mary Magdalene, Mary the mother of James, and Salome (Mark 16:1)
   c) Luke says "the women" (Luke 24:1)
   d) John says Mary Magdalene (John 20:1)

2. Who was at the tomb?
   a) Matthew says an angel came down, opened the tomb, then sat on the stone. His appearance was like lightning and he was dressed in white clothes (Matthew 28:2)
   b) Mark says a young man dressed in a white robe was sitting on the right (Mark 16:5)
   c) Luke says two men in clothes that gleamed like lightning stood beside them (the women) (Luke 24:4)
   d) John says two angels were seen at the head and foot of where Jesus had been laid. This was *after* the earlier trip and *after* Peter and John had visited (John 20:11,12)

Response to Contradictions

This is how similarities and differences of eyewitnesses can add depth and meaning to historical events (see p. 7). Each eyewitness, or those recording what other eyewitnesses said, focuses on a different part of the full picture, the part of particular interest to them. Yet when the entire story is read in chronological order, the gaps are filled in and this becomes a very complete story of the events of that day.

Chronological Account of the Resurrection

Women come to the tomb. When the Sabbath was over, Mary Magdalene, Mary the mother of James, and Salome bought spices so that they might go to anoint Jesus' body. Very early on the first day of the week, just after sunrise, they were on their way to the tomb, and they asked each other, "Who will roll the stone away from the entrance of the tomb?"

But when they looked up, they saw that the stone, which was very large, had already been rolled away. (See Matthew 28:1; Mark 16:1-4.)

Resurrection announced. As they entered the tomb, they saw a young man dressed in a white robe sitting on the right side, and they were alarmed. (See Mark 16:5.)

"Don't be alarmed," he said. "You are looking for Jesus the Nazarene, who was crucified. He has risen! He is not here. See the place where they laid him. But go, tell his disciples and Peter, 'He is going ahead of you into Galilee. There you will see him, just as he told you.'" (See Matthew 28:5-7.)

Women reminded of prophecy. While they were wondering about this, suddenly two men in clothes that gleamed like lightning stood beside them. In their fright the women bowed down to them. "Why do you look for the living among the dead?" the men questioned. "He is not here; he has risen! Remember how he told you, while he was still with you in Galilee: 'The Son of Man must be delivered into the hands of sinful men, be crucified and on the third day be raised again.'" Then they remembered his words. (See Luke 24:4-8.)

Women go away fearful. Trembling and bewildered, the women went out and fled from the tomb. They said nothing to anyone, because they were afraid.

Peter and John told. Mary of Magdala came running to Simon Peter and the other disciple, the one Jesus loved, and said, "They have taken the Lord out of the tomb, and we don't know where they have put him!" (John 20:2).

Peter and John view the tomb. So Peter and the other disciple started for the tomb. Both were running, but the other disciple outran Peter and reached the tomb first. He looked into the tomb and saw the strips of linen lying there, but he did not go in. Then Simon Peter arrived and went into the tomb. "He saw the strips of linen lying there, as well as the burial cloth that had been around Jesus' head. The cloth was folded up by itself, separate from the linen. Finally the other disciple, who had reached the tomb first, also went inside. He saw and believed. (They still did not understand from Scripture that Jesus had to rise from the dead.) Then the disciples went back to their homes" (John 20:3-10; see also Luke 24:12).

Jesus with Mary Magdalene. When Jesus rose early on the first day of the week, he appeared first to Mary Magdalene, out of whom he had driven seven demons (Mark 16:9). Mary stood outside the tomb crying. As she wept, she bent over to look into the tomb and saw two angels in white, seated where Jesus' body had been, one at the head and the other at the foot.

They asked her, "Woman, why are you crying?"

"They have taken my Lord away," she said, "and I don't know where they have put him." At this, she turned around and saw Jesus standing there, but she did not realize that it was Jesus.

"Woman," he said, "why are you crying? Who is it you are looking for?"

Thinking he was the gardener, she said, "Sir, if you have carried him away, tell me where you have put him, and I will get him."

Jesus said to her, "Mary."

She turned toward him and cried out in Aramaic, "Rabboni!" (which means Teacher). Jesus said, "Do not hold on to me, for I have not yet returned to the Father. Go instead to my brothers and tell them,

'I am returning to my Father and your Father, to my God and your God'" (John 20:11-17).

Jesus appears to women. So the women hurried away from the tomb, afraid yet filled with joy, and ran to tell his disciples. Suddenly Jesus met them. "Greetings," he said. They came to him, clasped his feet and worshiped him. Then Jesus said to them, "Do not be afraid. Go and tell my brothers to go to Galilee; there they will see me" (Matthew 28:8-10).[12]

Conclusions

The Gospel writers certainly had access to the eyewitnesses. The fundamentals of this account are sound in each gospel record: 1) Women went to the tomb, 2) they encountered angels, 3) the tomb was empty, 4) they were told Jesus had arisen from death, and 5) the disciples checked the tomb as well.

In a court of law, these fundamentals by key eyewitnesses would be irrefutable, especially when corroborated by the account of the Roman guard. The differences of the stories are easily accounted for simply by reviewing the similarities and differences of eyewitness accounts, which add credibility and clarity to a historical event. The chronology indicates no contradiction.

Other Suspected Contradictions

The Name of Nehemiah's Opponent?

The book of Nehemiah refers to Nehemiah's opponent using two names. Verse 2:19 uses the name "Geshem," while verse 6:6 refers to him as "Gashmu" (KJV, NASB). Which is right? As indicated on pages 9 and 10, it was not uncommon for people to have multiple names. In this particular case, however, the difference is based on the common usage of the Arabic speaking people, who typically end names with a "u," and the Aramaic–Hebrew speaking people whose names usually omit the short vowel endings. The book of Nehemiah uses the common Arab reference in one case and the common Hebrew reference in the other.

The Maniac(s) and Pigs of Gadara?

The gospels of Matthew, Mark, and Luke all record an incident of Jesus healing the maniac(s) of Gennesaret (Matthew 8:30-34; Mark 5:11-14; Luke 8:27-33). There are two potential problems. First, Matthew indicates there were *two* demon-possessed maniacs, while Mark and Luke indicate only one. This is easily explained by the importance of similarities and differences of eyewitnesses. In the case of Mark and Luke, it is likely that one individual was more prominent and memorable. Certainly their accounts don't exclude a second person.

The second issue is location: Gadara (or Gerasa)? Matthew 8:28 refers to the people as Gadarenes, but they lived southeast of the Sea of Galilee. This region is far from the sea, and it would be impossible for the swine to run off a cliff into the sea as indicated. The people in the general region, however, were still referred to as Gadarenes based on the prominent city of Gadara (or Gerasa). Therefore, the people in the region were accurately called Gadarenes, although the actual place of the swine running into the sea was at Gennesaret.

Jehoiachin's Curse?

One of the most amazing contradictions centers on the curse God placed on Jehoiachin in Jeremiah 22:30. God declared that Jehoiachin, a king of Judah, was to be considered childless, that "none of his descendents would sit on the throne of David." Yet he is included in the genealogy in Matthew 1:11,12.

So how could Jesus be proclaimed as the ultimate king without contradicting Jeremiah 22:30? The answer is that God's unique plan included having the Holy Spirit "overshadow" Mary to conceive Jesus. No human male was necessary.

Jesus had the unique position of being born of a human mother and the Spirit of a perfect God. But through the male line He did inherit His lineage as king.

Jairus' Daughter?

There appear to be two different versions of the incident of Jesus being called upon to heal Jairus' daughter. Matthew 9:18,19 indicates that the daughter is already dead. A "ruler" came to Jesus and said, "My daughter has just died." However both Mark 5:22,23 and Luke 8:41,42 indicate that Jairus himself came to Jesus and that his daughter was *dying*.

Applying the approach mentioned on pp. 14-15, we need to look for a reasonable hypothesis that makes sense according to two different eyewitnesses. In this case the most plausible situation is fairly simple. Mark and Luke recorded a first visit by Jairus. Jesus was being detained by a throng of people (Mark 5:23-34; Luke 8:43-48). And, upon a *second* visit, Jairus announced that his child had died.

Why Does Jesus Quote Isaiah Differently?

Matthew 13:13-15 and John 12:37-40 indicate two quotations by Jesus of Isaiah 53:1 and 6:9. Why are they not exactly the same?

It's important to realize that the use of paraphrase was as prevalent then as it is today. Jesus, in speaking to different audiences at different points in time, may have had a reason for different emphases.

Staff or Staffs? Shoes or Sandals?

Some are concerned with an alleged contradiction in Matthew 10:9,10 and Mark 6:8,9. Matthew indicates that Jesus commanded His disciples to minister without *staffs* and not to take shoes. Mark says that they take only a staff and wear only sandals. It seems like a contradiction until we recognize some key elements of the culture of the day. The plural usage of the word "staffs" was generally regarded as preparation for fighting, whereas a single staff was regarded as needed for walking. Similarly is the difference in the words for shoes (hypodema) versus sandals (sin-dal), which was regarded as a much simpler form of clothing. It is fairly obvious that Jesus was instructing His disciples not to take anything more than that which was required.

A Sign or No Sign?

Jesus was disturbed that religious leaders demanded a "sign" to "test" Him. Mark indicates that no sign will be given (Mark 8:11,12). Matthew and Luke indicate that no sign will be given *except* the sign of Jonah being in the belly of a large fish for three days and nights (Matthew 12:38,39; Luke 11:29,30). Are these contradictory?

Consider that Jesus may have made this comment more than once. His indication in Mark may have stopped short of mentioning the "sign of Jonah." After all, the point of the story was to criticize the seeking of "signs" in general.

How Many Donkeys?

In Matthew 21:2 we find two donkeys mentioned in preparation for Jesus' entrance into Jerusalem on Palm Sunday—a donkey and her colt. Yet in Mark 11:2 and Luke 19:30, only a young male donkey is mentioned. Why would these accounts differ?

All three gospels agree that Jesus rode into Jerusalem on a young donkey, or foal (polos in Greek).[13] So the "contradiction" concerns only the second donkey and whether or not it was male or female.

Perhaps the most significant point is Matthew's reference to prophecy (Zechariah 9:9). The prophet Zechariah's words indicate that the Messiah would arrive on a donkey (*h mor* in Greek).[13] On the issue of a second donkey, it would be common for a foal to follow its mother, which makes sense in the context of Jesus riding "a colt, the foal of a donkey" on Palm Sunday.

What Color Robe?

Sometimes supposed contradictions come down to details that are hard to understand. Matthew 27:28 indicates that Jesus was stripped then given a scarlet robe. In John 19:2 the robe Jesus wore was purple. First, we need to realize that even today differences in shades of color can be disputable, perhaps in the same way turquoise and blue fall into similar categories. In ancient times, people gave the word "purple" to any color that had red in it. Another issue is that "scarlet" is commonly associated with military (Roman) colors, which would have likely been associated with the clothing put on Jesus.

A Sign or No Sign
for Pharisees?

Why did Jesus criticize the Pharisees for asking him for a sign from heaven? (See Mark 8:11-13.) Then, in Matthew 12:38,39, it's indicated that the only sign of a Messiah would be the symbol of Jonah being three days in the belly of a large fish, which parallels Jesus' death (Matthew 12:38,39). Was not the resurrection of Jesus, as a model of Jonah, a sign?

Further analysis of the intent of Jesus makes this contradiction disappear. The intention of Jesus was to criticize the Pharisees for requesting an *immediate* "sign," as in a magical demonstration. Jesus wanted their focus to be on the longer-term sign of the death and resurrection that was tied to the model of Jonah.

Peter's Denial and the Rooster Crowing?

Typical of the minor contradictions some make about the gospel accounts is the issue of Peter denying Jesus three times in relationship to how many times the rooster crowed. For example, Matthew states that Jesus said, "This very night, before the rooster crows, you will disown me three times" (26:34). Mark adds a little more detail, saying that the rooster will crow twice before Peter disowns him three times (14:30). Luke tends to agree with an abbreviated version of Matthew. So what is the contradiction? If the rooster crowed twice, it certainly crowed once. Again, the strength of similarities and differences of eyewitnesses in their accounts adds details that do not rule out each other.

What Was the Wording on the Cross?

Another alleged point of contradiction is the precise wording on the cross of Jesus. First consider the different wordings given by the four gospel writers (see next page). Why are these different?

The first, perhaps most important, clue is given by John. He stated that the message was written in three languages, apparently to be understood by the many passersby of different cultures. It was written in Latin, the language Pilate would have known; in Greek, a common language used in Palestine; and in Hebrew or Aramaic (John uses the word *Hebraisti*, which is a dialect of Aramaic).[14]

Wording Variations on the Cross

Matthew 27:37: "This is Jesus, the king of the Jews."

Mark 15:26: "The king of the Jews."

Luke 23:38: "This is the king of the Jews."

John 19:19: "Jesus of Nazareth, the king of the Jews."

The first hypothesis is that gospel writers chose to write the essence of the message. But, more likely, the three versions varied slightly. The simplistic versions in Mark or Luke may have been

written in Latin, which would be understandable to the Romans in the area. Pilate may have added the name "Jesus" to the Aramaic version since it may have been more appropriate to the locals who followed Jesus. Some scholars believe Matthew's original gospel was written in Aramaic. Quite possibly Pilate decided, *after* writing the message in Latin, to add the city to which Jesus belonged (Nazareth), which would be relevant to the local people.

How Did Judas Iscariot Die?

Matthew 27:3-5 says Judas, filled with remorse after betraying Jesus, hung himself. Yet Acts 1:18 indicates that Judas "fell headlong" and his intestines gushed out. By visiting the area traditionally identified with Judas' death, you will realize that both accounts may be right. A number of trees with dry, weak branches overhang great cliffs. It takes very little to believe that Judas hung himself, but the branch broke and he fell to his death.

Common Questions

Wouldn't a loving God allow good people into heaven?

Many people believe that living a good life and being kind to others is the way to heaven. Naturally, they are thinking of a "good" life in terms of our distorted human view; and such a life is far from God's standard. The Bible says that the *only* way to God the Father in heaven is through Jesus Christ (John 14:6). So will loving and "good" people who don't accept Jesus go to hell? Yes—but how can they be truly good if they reject the love of God's Son, Jesus, who died for them?

God will allow perfectly good people into heaven. But His standard of goodness is the perfection of His Son Jesus. Hence, there is simply no other way to come to Him except through Jesus—let alone the fact that every sin of mind or body we commit removes us further from Jesus' perfection (Matthew 5:28,29; Romans 3:22,23).

Everyone is imperfect, but the good news is that God has provided Jesus as a perfect sacrifice for us. He is our way to heaven. Not accepting God's gift of love and forgiveness through Jesus, despite the Holy Spirit's prompting, is unforgivable (Mark 3:29).

How can we ensure the right relationship so we can go to heaven?

When Jesus said that not all who use His name will enter heaven, He was referring to people who think using His name, along with rules and rituals, is the key to heaven (see Matthew 7:21-23). A *relationship* with God is *not* based on rituals or rules. It's based on grace, forgiveness, and true communion with God.

Prayer for Eternal Life with God

Dear God, I believe You sent Your Son, Jesus, to die for my sins so I can be forgiven. I'm sorry for my sins. I want to live the rest of my life the way You want me to. Please put Your Spirit in my life to direct me. Amen.

Then What?

People who sincerely take these steps become members of God's family of believers. New freedom and strength is available through prayer and obedience to God's will. Your new relationship can be strengthened by:

- Finding a *Bible-based church* that you like and attend regularly.
- Setting aside time each day to pray and read the Bible.
- Locating other Christians to spend time with on a regular basis.

God's Promises to Believers

Today

But seek first his kingdom and his righteousness, and all these things (e.g., things to satisfy all your needs) will be given to you as well.
Matthew 6:33

Eternity

Whoever believes in the Son has eternal life, but whoever rejects the Son will not see life, for God's wrath remains on him.
John 3:36

Once we develop an eternal perspective, even the greatest problems on earth fade in significance.

Notes

Note: The author does not agree with *all* authors below on *all* viewpoints. Each reference has some findings worthy of consideration. (*"Test everything"* —1 Thessalonians 5:21).

1. *Webster's II New Riverside University Dictionary,* Boston, MA: The Riverside Publishing Company, 1984.

2. Muncaster, Ralph O. *Can Archaeology Prove the Old Testament?* Examine the Evidence Series. Eugene OR: Harvest House, 2000.

3. Muncaster, Ralph O. *Science: Was the Bible Ahead of Its Time?* Examine the Evidence Series. Eugene OR: Harvest House, 2000.

4. Elwell, Walter A., ed., *Evangelical Dictionary of Theology.* Grand Rapids, MI: Baker Book House Co., 1984.

5. Gardner, Joseph L. ed. director. *Reader's Digest Who's Who in the Bible.* Pleasantville, NY: Reader's Digest Association, Inc., 1994.

6. Elwell, *Evangelical Dictionary,* p. 464.

7. Youngblood, Ronald F. *New Illustrated Bible Dictionary.* Nashville, TN: Nelson, 1995, p. 879.

8. Archer, Gleason L. *Encyclopedia of Bible Difficulties.* Grand Rapids, MI: Zondervan Publishing House, 1982, p. 316.

9. McRay, John, *Archaeology and the New Testament.* Grand Rapids, MI: Baker Book House, 1991, p. 17.

10. Archer, Gleason L. *Encyclopedia of Bible Difficulties.*

11. Hoehner, Harold W. *Chronological Aspects of the Life of Christ.* Grand Rapids, MI: Zondervan Publishing House, 1977.

12. Smith, F. LaGard. *The Daily Bible in Chronological Order.* Eugene, OR: Harvest House, 1984.

13. *The Complete Word Study of the Old Testament.* Chattanooga, TN: AMG Publishers, 1991.

14. Archer, *Encyclopedia of Bible Difficulties,* p. 346.

Bibliography

Cloud, David W. *Things Hard to Be Understood, a Handbook of Biblical Difficulties.* Oak Harbour, WA: Way of Life Literature, 1996.

The Complete Word Study of the Old Testament. Chattanooga, TN: AMG Publishers, 1991.

Geisler, Norman, Ph.D., and Ron Brooks. *When Skeptics Ask.* Grand Rapids, MI: Baker Books, 1990.

Life Application Bible, Wheaton, IL: Tyndale House Publishers, 1991.

Lockyer, Herbert, *All the Miracles of the Bible.* Grand Rapids, MI: Zondervan Publishing House, 1961.

Mc Dowell, Josh, and Bill Wilson. *A Ready Defense.* San Bernadino, CA: Here's Life Publishers, Inc., 1990.

Muncaster, Ralph O. *Can You Trust the Bible?* Examine the Evidence Series. Eugene OR: Harvest House, 2000.

Muncaster, Ralph O. *Does the Bible Predict the Future?* Examine the Evidence Series. Eugene OR: Harvest House, 2000.

Walvoord, John F. *The Prophecy Knowledge Handbook.* Wheaton, IL: Victor Books, 1990.